Bernie Sanders attended
Brooklyn College
for one year before
transferring to the
University of Chicago,
where he earned a B.A.
in political science in
1964.

PLATE 1

Bernie often wears a traditional business suit and tie with a small gold lapel pin that identifies him as a U.S. Senator. During the March 9, 2016 televised Democratic debate, it was the color of his suit that caused the biggest controversy when viewers argued via social media over its actual color. Was it brown, blue, or black? Staff insiders assured the public it was, indeed, blue.

PLATE 2

Bernie played
basketball in his
youth and still enjoys
shooting hoops. In fact,
following the news of
his Democratic New
Hampshire primary
win, the senator joined
his adult sons and some
of his grandkids for
some fun on the court.

PLATE 3

Sanders was a track
star at James Madison
High School in his
native Brooklyn. He
was captain of both his
track and cross country
teams and known as a
fierce competitor. The
school's 1959 yearbook
dubbed Sanders' track
team "one of the best in
Madison's history."

PLATE 4

During his college years, Bernie was very active in several peace and antiwar movements, as well as civil rights and economic justice organizations. He participated in the "March on Washington" in 1963, where Dr. Martin Luther King Jr. delivered his stirring "I Have a Dream" speech.

PLATE 5

Bernie left Brooklyn behind to embrace the lifestyle in Vermont. This outfit shows him as a true "Vermonter," ready to hit the slopes or to sit down and enjoy a stack of hotcakes topped with Vermont's delicious maple syrup.

PLATE 6

In 1987, while mayor of Burlington, Sanders recorded a folk album, "We Shall Overcome," with 30 Vermont singers and musicians. Recently Sanders joked, "If people are thinking of voting for me for my musical capabilities not the right reason. I have other attributes. Carrying a tune is not one of them."

PLATE 7

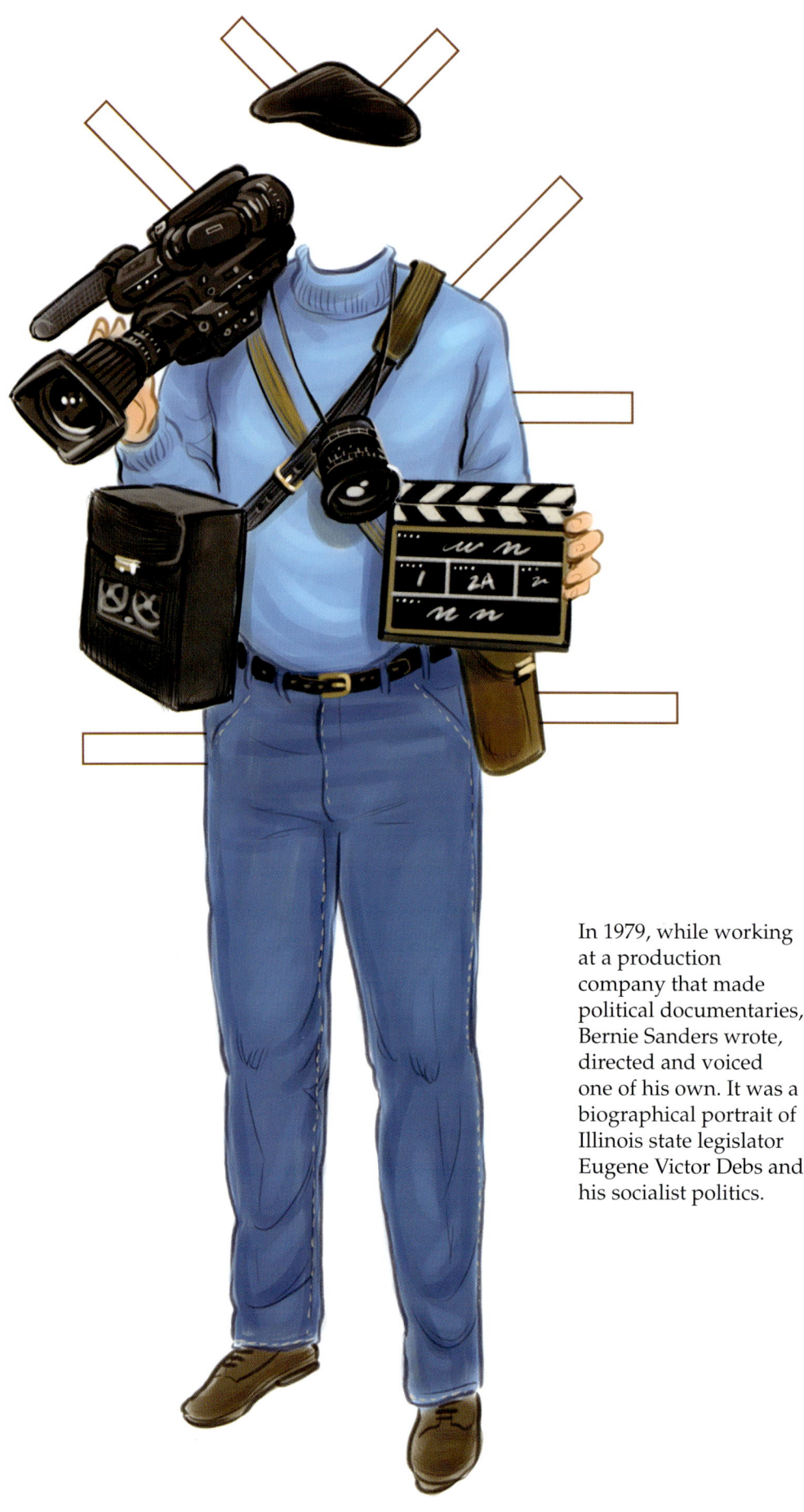

In 1979, while working at a production company that made political documentaries, Bernie Sanders wrote, directed and voiced one of his own. It was a biographical portrait of Illinois state legislator Eugene Victor Debs and his socialist politics.

PLATE 8

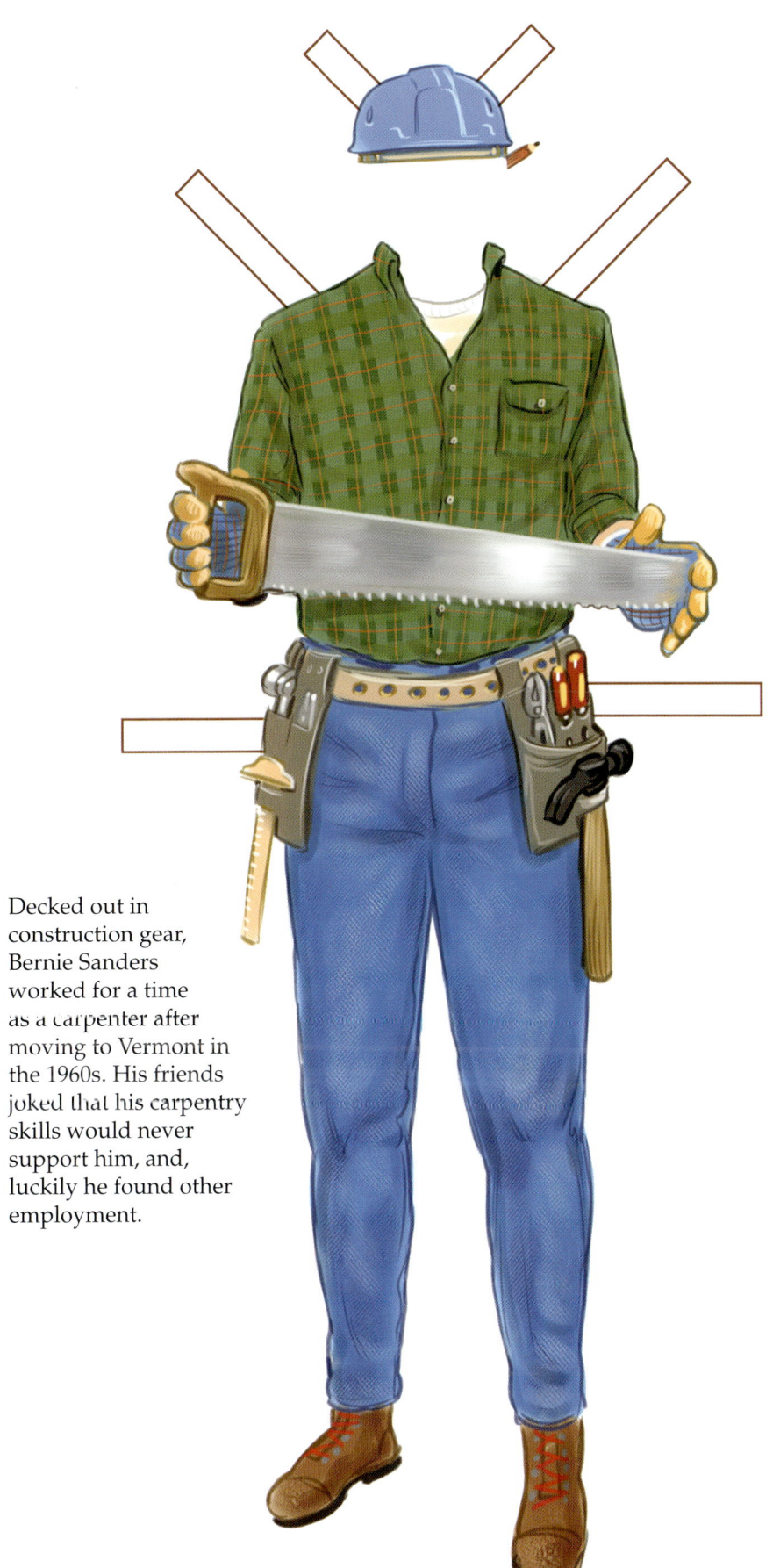

Decked out in construction gear, Bernie Sanders worked for a time as a carpenter after moving to Vermont in the 1960s. His friends joked that his carpentry skills would never support him, and, luckily he found other employment.

PLATE 9

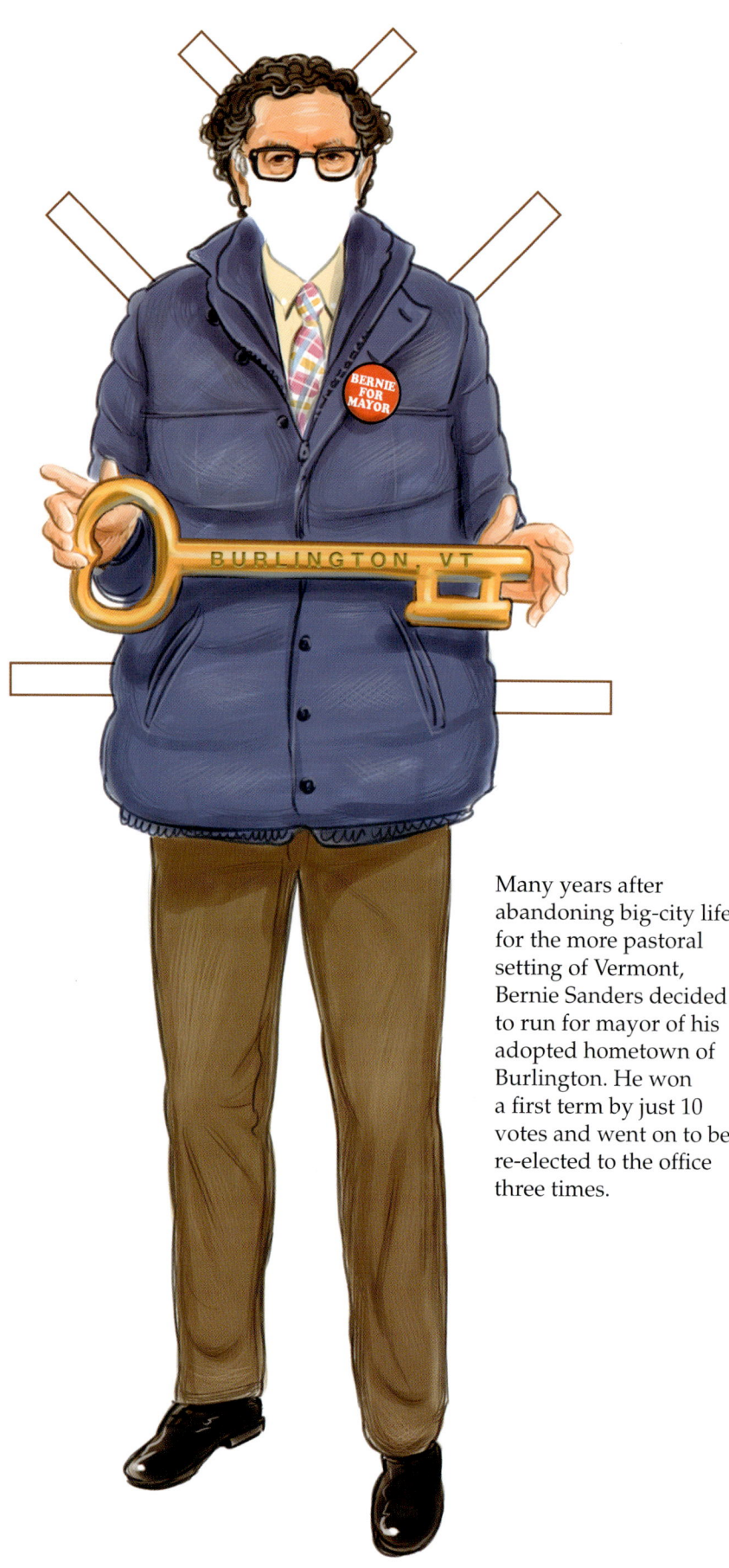

Many years after abandoning big-city life for the more pastoral setting of Vermont, Bernie Sanders decided to run for mayor of his adopted hometown of Burlington. He won a first term by just 10 votes and went on to be re-elected to the office three times.

PLATE 10

Senator Sanders gave an 8½-hour filibuster in December 2010 against the reinstatement of the George W. Bush tax cuts, claiming that they would benefit only higher-income Americans. *#FiliBernie* became the world's largest Twitter trend at that time.

PLATE 11

This "Feel the Bern" apron is the perfect complement to the casual attire the candidate might wear on a rare day off from campaigning. Although not much of a foodie, Sanders has admitted that he's "pretty good on the grill" and that pork chops are one of his favorite meals.

PLATE 12

Bernie Sanders believes that all Americans deserve the opportunity to receive an affordable, quality education. He has sponsored bills to make public colleges and universities tuition-free, as well as to drastically reduce interest rates on student-loan debt.

PLATE 13

On February 6, 2016, Bernie Sanders stepped off the campaign trail and dressed in costume to poke fun at himself by appearing alongside comedic actor/writer Larry David in a *Saturday Night Live* skit. David's likeness to Sanders had the Internet buzzing both before and after the presidential candidate's appearance.

Plate 14

For a brief moment, Bernie Sanders was "Birdie" Sanders. When a small bird landed on the podium during his speech at a rally in Portland, Oregon, the senator quipped: "I know it doesn't look like it, but that bird is really a dove asking us for world peace. No more wars!" And for the doting grandfather of seven, that is an extremely important goal.

PLATE 15

Bernie Sanders as
superhero—prepared
to do battle with his
opponents to win
the 2016 Presidential
election.

PLATE 16